GARDEN ReVISIONS

Poems for
Gardeners True & Honest

John C. Streed

Illustrations by
John and Kim Aldrich

Murray Garden Press
Excelsior, Minnesota 55331

John C. Streed

Garden Revisions: Poems for Gardeners True and Honest

ISBN 0-9639126-0-7

Printed and bound in the United States of America

9 8 7 6 5 4 3 2 1

FOR THE FLOWERS IN MY GARDEN

Alec

Kyle

Drew

Imy

Preface

Gardening attracts people, all kinds of people. The attraction is so widespread, so compelling, so democratic, that one must conclude the roots are very deep within. Perhaps there are even genetic elements to the matter. We yearn to garden as we yearn to explore, to inquire, to mate. Whatever the case, the gardener of today is of honorable lineage stretching back through generations of artists and farmers to whoever it was who first pulled some leaves out of the way in order to better view a bloom, and then pulled out some nearby plants in order that the flower have an easier time of growing.

The gardener is not exactly a farmer although there are farmer gardeners. Nor is the gardener simply an exterior decorator although there are garden designers who are no more than that. The gardener plants and grows and arranges and admires with satisfactions and frustrations not easily analyzed. Gardeners are, as artists must be, sub-creators. They do not make something out of nothing. They can only take elements that already exist and play around with them, provide conditions that promote growth, cause plants to increase, rearrange them, and be pleased (or displeased) with the results. That is why gardening is, as it were, happy work. It can be hard. A day in the garden, especially for those who can only get out there once in a while, can be an interesting physiological experience, but it is gratifying, and it is fun.

There is a variation of Parkinson's Law that prevails in gardening. Necessary gardening responsibilities and plans—the things you have to do and the things you want to do—always exceed the available time and space. Gardeners are always running behind. To paraphrase Browning, their "reach always exceeds their grasp, or what's a garden for?" This is one of the reasons why it is said that, unlike houses, gardens are always in transition. There is always a sense that something more ought to be done. But it is not an unpleasant sense, else we would not put up with it. We would go into ceramics or collecting or TV sports. But we do put up with it, and it makes for a better life.

The poems in this collection are intended to celebrate a few of the elements of that better life: the pleasures, the follies, the frustrations, and, certainly, the mysteries. These poems are for gardeners, however large or small their gardens might be, and for those who would be gardeners if they had the opportunity.

J. Streed
Excelsior, Minnesota
1993

(Some) Credit Where (More) Credit Is Due

These poems were at first the work of the author alone, and there was much lacking. (I am embarrassed to think of how much.) Due, however, to the efforts of several people, the poems are now, both individually and collectively, much improved in form and appearance. Honesty, no less than courtesy, requires that credit be given for that improvement. Eleanor Woodey and Mary Skoy found errors and weaknesses of all kinds in the first drafts and, since the author kept revising, in the drafts that followed. Their high standards fortunately prevailed. The whole book would have been a joke were it not for them. John and Kim Aldrich patiently sketched and erased and sketched again. Their talent is obvious, but they cannot be held accountable for everything. The observant reader will notice three illustrations (21, 30, and 43) inferior in conception and execution. These are the work of the author. Cover design by the old gardener. Peggie Carley processed and revised over and over again with remarkable patience, and then brought the words and the illustrations together on the page with remarkable skill. Linda Hanner guided the project from inception to book store. I doubt that any of these people understand how much I needed their help and how much help they gave. But I know, and I am very grateful. I thank them here.

JCS

The Poems

A Sonnet for Gardeners

When musing through the hours for that which could,

While factions strive, and conflicts ever reign,

Promote the needful cause of social good,

My thoughts will oft return to gardeners plain.

Midst fashion vain and scandaled public eye,

Midst TV guile and market search for gold,

The gardener's quiet work does pacify

And soothe the tired heart with practice old.

Most rare the scene of brawling garden club,

Of matron fierce, or plantsman shouting doom.

No bloody bruise, at worst a quiet snub

When judges praise the neighbor's winning bloom.

Due honor, then, to those who, stiff with toil,

Do show how well to live this mortal coil.

Ordering from the Catalogs

My caution goes numb when the catalogs come.
No way will it end for the good.
Cold winter without, but the spring pages shout,
"You better buy more than you should."

Some flowers, some seed: I just check what I need.
The total? Five hundred and ten!
A terrible blow. So back I must go.
The list must be pruned and then . . .

It's still way too high. I almost can cry.
The visions of glory are fading.
Cross out and erase. A perennial case
Of not enough cash. How degrading.

The list now is brief after pain and much grief.
The numbers, though, still wreck my budget.
Much more must be cut. I economize, but
The truth . . . well, I'm going to fudge it.

For I cannot say no to the flowers that glow
On the page and then after, the garden.
So what if I blunder? The balance goes under.
I'll look to the bank for a pardon.

All shame be to them if their view is so grim
That money they count more than beauty.
As for me, I must grow every flower I know,
For that, I believe, is my duty.

The Many and the Few

What makes a flower special, if you are ignorant,
Is seldom little more than it grow up different.

Old fashioned shape and beauty, plain color, charm, and grace,
These matter very little within the market place.

What there is much sought after is that the thing be new.
So long as it's the first, almost anything will do.

Pick any flower growing; I care not what it be.
A new and different version will almost certainly

Be hailed as a winner by the authorities
Who mostly pay attention to this year's novelties.

If Dante's Rose Celestial were focused in one bloom,
The market would require a variation soon.

(With flowers as with people, there're few things quite so drear
As going out of style; that prospect gives no cheer.)

But though the many scurry to ride the latest fad,
There are those gardeners honest—if you are one, be glad—

Who need no status blooms, who the fashions new ignore.
They like the old familiar, the same thing evermore.

Secure in patterns lasting, no need to new things try,
They grow and grow again, and let the world go by.

Too Soon

My garden always is full to the edge,
Like yours, I'm sure, and it's hard to wedge
Any more stuff within the borders,
So there's not much use in placing orders
For plants and things to add to where
I've already filled my irregular square.

Thus you can see how pleased last spring
I was to discover some room for things,
Lots of room, as a matter of fact,
And I prepared myself to promptly act
By getting the shovel, a pail of sand,
Some flowers I needed, some compost, and
I began to dig in those happy spaces,
Anxious to fill the empty places
That strangely enough I had forgotten
Were all around my little plot in
Which I thought I had planted all
I could possibly plant when I quit last fall.

But what a surprise when the shovel slid
Smoothly through the dirt that hid,
Too late to see, some bulbs expensive
Now sliced in two. Thus apprehensive
I moved with care to an open spot
Where I certainly hoped that there was not
Anything lurking in the ground below
To be cut in half by shovel or hoe.

But, alas, again, decapitation
Of a slow growing piece of vegetation.
Once more I tried, most careful now.

Ouch! One was two. It was then clear how
There was open ground
Amongst those flowers all around.

It was open only because the growing
Was not above the surface showing,
And the spaces open that pleased me so
Were really my plants incognito.

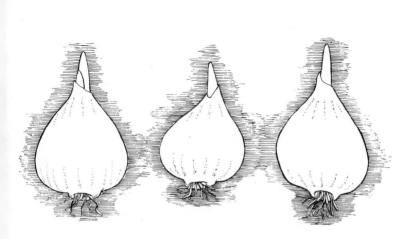

Garden Work

It's Saturday and I am free
To work the whole day through.
I have a list of jobs for me,
Those things that I must do.

To fix the edging, that is first.
That must be done today.
It absolutely looks the worst.
No more can I delay.

But while I'm here, I think I might
As well divide that phlox.
For it will make a pretty sight
If moved here by these rocks.

Some compost rich will help a lot.
I've got some really near.
But oh, the bin is mostly rot.
I'll fix it while I'm here.

I ought to weed, since I am close,
This bed a little while.
Don't want my garden looking gross.
That's really not my style.

These hosta now are really big.
They're taking too much room.
It won't take long to quickly dig
Them up before they bloom.

Yet, how the time so quickly flies.
Now lunch is calling me.
When I get back, I'll organize
And most efficient be.

Oh, yes, that edging's still to do.
It will not go away.
Don't think that I've forgotten it.
I've still got half a day.

But maybe I should put some more
Astilbe in the shade.
And when I finish that small chore,
I'll try to find the spade.

And now, you edging, here I come.
This is, for you, the end.
But first I'll quick trim up this mum,
And others neatly tend.

Now here I see that mulch I must
Put round these tender plants.
The ground's so dry it's almost dust.
To wait I really can't.

Some water then is what they need.
On that these plants depend.
But quickly now with careful speed
The hose I've got to mend.

It's getting dark. My back is sore.
I've had enough today.
The edging has survived once more.
There's nothing I can say.

Dividing and Labeling Perennials

These clumps are big. Time to divide.
First split them up. Then spread them wide.

The job is tough. Don't bother me.
I've got to think. I've got to see.

Now little plants are all around.
All neatly settled on the ground.

But great the danger, great the risk.
Catastrophe if stuff gets mixed.

These labels here; those labels there.
Divisions set. Now take a care.

This pile's safe. And that one, too.
But what were these? Don't they look new?

Before I mark—oops, my foot just moved
These three or four. Things aren't improved.

Were they from there? Or were they . . . here
By this pile? I'm not quite clear . . .

This looks like those . . . I think, well, maybe . . .
No, it must go . . . Ah . . . It's with this baby

Here . . . Unless it came from over there . . .
But these look like . . . No . . . This isn't fair!

Who moved those four? There by that brick?
I know I put . . . Is this a trick?

What label should . . . I'm lost . . . confess . . .
Can't keep them straight. Now it's a mess.

I think I'll plant this year, I guess,
A new variety named "Misc."

Too Many Carrots

Catalogs around me spread.
Getting fuzzy in the head.
Time to pick for summer sowing
All the veggies I'll be growing.
Favorites old, and offerings new,
Choices many. What to do?
Time it takes. More than a night.
Mostly things will work out right.
Choices soon become clear cut,
But the carrots drive me nuts.
Why so many orange roots?
Surely no one ever puts
Fifty kinds of carrot seed
In the ground to thin and weed.

Big Imperator is king,
Good for easy harvesting.
Danvers is a breed to please.
Little Amsterdams just tease.
Nantes stout seem not to end.
Paris Market sets a trend.
Last to name is Chantenay.
That's enough is what I say.

Each of these has sired dozens.
That's too many carrot cousins.
What to order from this bunch?
Not a clue, not a hunch.
This, it seems, is where I'm at.
Carrot thin or carrot fat?
Carrot short or carrot tall?
Really, I don't care at all.

Folly

Need to move a giant stone.
Need to do it all alone.

Not a job that I will shirk.
Careful, though. It's risky work.

Always there's a chance of harm.
Twist a leg or bruise an arm.

Worst of all the back to strain.
Foolish risk for little gain.

Many years my back was strong.
Chance it now? Would be wrong.

Get a shovel, wiggle, pry.
Just a little extra try.

Now I need an iron bar.
In the shed, but that's too far.

Got to hurry, got to move.
Got some landscape to improve.

Shovel handle's strong enough.
Muscle down, that's the stuff.

One last push and—Oops! CRACK!
There goes shovel and my back.

Losing Tools

Same old song.
Trowel's gone.

Look around
On the ground.

Here and there,
Everywhere.

By the knife?
By my life,

That's gone, too!
What to do?

What the heck.
Round the neck

Need a string.
Tie each thing.

Gardeners' way.
Price to pay.

Worth it, though.
Helps things grow.

Too Late

The UPS just pulled away.
He left some cartons here to stay.

My tulip bulbs and daffodils
For autumn planting, springtime thrills.

Now warmly shines September sun.
There's lots of time to get things done.

It may be late, but still I need
To scatter on the lawn some seed.

And at the moment, shrubbery prune.
That's sure to take an afternoon.

And for the fire, wood to stack.
Look, here's October. Fall is back.

Must get those bulbs all in the ground
Before the frost comes back around.

But weekend time so quickly passes.
Now brown the leaves and brown the grasses.

Then rake those leaves, and tote that bale.
Prepare some mulch for winter's gale.

For sure next week those bulbs go in, though
First I better fix the window.

Now grim November cold does harden
Deep the dirt in all the garden.

But plant those bulbs, I must, I will.
Plant while my fingers function still.

And now to hack the ground so frozen.
A better time I should have chosen.

But I've been busy every moment
While all those bulbs have lain there dormant.

Tomorrow, though, this race I'll win.
Tomorrow morn those bulbs go in.

What's that I see outside? Oh, no!
Here comes December's blowing snow.

Blizzard howling round the corners.
Too late, alas, my bulbs are goners.

JCS

Lord of the Green

All praise to thee, thou flat green god,
Worshipful stretch of weed free sod.

No pagan dandelion shrine
Where heathen roots deep intertwine

With fescue pure and Kentucky blue.
Thou sward of hosts, we worship you.

We view thy verdant robe with rapture.
We hail thy even monoculture.

Your psalms sing forth in scripture annual,
Thy word to read in lawn care manual.

To serve thee best, we soak and spray
With potions strong to keep away

All wicked weeds from thy pure bosom.
Yea, this, our suburbs' catechism.

And woe to them who thee neglect,
Who think they need not genuflect

To custom strong and practice holy.
They'll suffer loss for being lowly.

Green mantled deity, giver of status,
This truth is sure: no lunch is gratis.

For thy rich blessing, we give to thee
Our tithe substantial, full willingly.

Take, we pray, our money, our time,
And whilst thou lives, our peace of mind.

Creeping Charlie

My lawn, how nice,
It spreads afar.
The weeds are few and foreign.
Some work, I know,
To keep it so
In pleasing green decorum.

Vigilance is
Necessary,
Else weeds will make it cruder.
But dig and pull
And rake and mow
Will conquer the intruder.

Grass, crab and quack,
Some Lamb's Ear, too.
Maybe oats and barley.
But the one I fear
The most of all
Is swiftly Creeping Charlie.

Inch by inch
He creeps apace,
If I'm awake or sleeping.
Nothing known
Can bring a halt
To Mr. Charlie Creeping.

Charlie Creeping,
Creeping Charlie,
The plant that conquers all.
Charlie, Charlie,
Strong and bold,
Summer, spring, and fall.

Charlie Creeping,
Creeping Charlie.
I'm glad you stay outdoors.
Charlie Creeping,
Creeping Charlie,
Soon my lawn is yours.

Creeping Charlie,
Creeping Charlie Charlie,
Charlie Creeping Creeping Charlie.
CreepingCharlieCreepingCharlieCreeping
CreepingCharlieCharlieCreepingCharlieCreeping
charliecreepingcharliecreepingcharliecreepingcharliecreep
creepingcharliecreepingcharliecreepingcharliecreepingcharliecreep
eepingcharliecreepingcharliecreepingcharliecreepingcharliecreepingcharliecr
pingcharliecreepingcharliecreepingcharliecreepingcharliecreepingcharliecree
ngcharliecreepingcharliecreepingcharliecreepingcharliecreepingcharliecreepi
gcharliecreepingcharliecreepingcharliecreepingcharliecreepingcharliecreepin
liecreepingcharliecreepingcharliecreepingcharliecreepingcharliecreepingchal
gcharliecreepingcharliecreepingcharliecreepingcharliecreepingcharliecreepin
liecreepingcharliecreepingcharliecreepingcharliecreepingcharliecreepingchar
gcharliecreepingcharliecreepingcharliecreepingcharliecreepingcharliecreepin
liecreepingcharliecreepingcharliecreepingcharliecreepingcharliecreepingchar
gcharliecreepingcharliecreepingcharliecreepingcharliecreepingcharliecreepin

Wetlands

Views of the Man down the Street upon Hearing That a
Building Site That He Had Purchased for Investment
Purposes Is Located in an Area Designated as Wetlands

"Wetlands! That's not wetlands. That's always been dry there.
Why, that's dry even when it's flooded all around here.
What cattails? Oh those. First time I've ever seen them there.
Must have blown in last year. Too dry for them to grow much.
Water? That little bit in the corner?
By the swamp? That always dries up in the summer.
Surprised it's still there. That's this freak weather.
Usually never even gets muddy. Woodducks, maybe,
Only kind of duck lives there. Well, if it rains all summer,
Sure you see mallards. But that's very unusual.
A little fill in the main part
Will improve drainage.
Better for wildlife downstream.
Great location for a nice house.
Natural area all around.
Going to keep it that way."

The Winners

Now who can doubt the truth of history's wondrous lesson
That humankind is best; our modest, true confession.

All "red in tooth and claw." That's nature's way of life.
"Survival of the fittest." Made are we for strife.

Those old Victorian creeds explain our species' climb.
How evolution's progress has brought us to our prime.

We met the challenge grim of nature fierce and wild.
And thus we reign today, the planet's favored child.

Now lords of all creation, ruling world wide.
No beast can match our wit. No error dim our pride,

Save in our garden cozy, yea, our modern Eden.
For there the beasts are winning; there we have been beaten.

The woodchuck, for example, has no fear of us.
Why should he? For he knows all we can do is cuss

The morning after he has hit the smorgasbords.
Raccoon, his striped partner, like the locust hordes

Has cleaned up all leftovers, left the field bare.
In case they missed a sprout, here comes the hungry hare.

Pray, don't one beauty slight, the gentle, trembling doe.
In search of lunches free, there's nowhere she won't go.

Of rodents, quick to gnaw, there is no end in sight.
Let's face it. Evolution's left us in a plight.

For in our little garden, where with loving care
We plant our seeds and bulbs to grow up strong and fair,

Our species rage in vain. Quite impotent are we.
And there the lesser creatures boast the victory.

The Triumph of Progress

I am not dumb. My end will come
Cowering in a garden bunker.
No coward, me, but finally
Progress forced me there to hunker.

Technology, as all can see,
Often takes the wrong direction.
And it's been hard within the yard.
There are grounds for my dejection.

The sounds of war which some ignore
Loudly echo through the nation.
The signal clear is one to fear:
Garden tool escalation.

The first attack, a long time back.
Heavy armor gained the field.
Machines to mow the grass we grow.
'Gainst that foe we had no shield.

Next weapons light joined in the fight.
Cursèd be the loud leaf blowers.
The snarling new weed whippers, too,
Joined forces with those mowers.

Then into view came ordnance new,
Pruners, shredders, used with zeal.
Without, within, a mighty din.
Never will my spirit heal.

The end, I fear, will soon be here;
Few the tools lacking power.
When trowels small have motors all,
That will be the final hour.

The eager crowd cheers progress loud,
That swelling, subtle villainy
Which with it brings on iron wings
The garden's rude cacophony.

Dreaming

The bookstores at the mall,
The local library,
I browse within them all,
A monied gardenry.

There the great estates
Where gods of wealth have smiled.
There statues patinate
Guard pools richly tiled.

There ivy ramparts bold
Over beds of color tower.
There arbors wide and old
Shade the mossy, ferny bower.

There vistas lead the eye
To mountain ranges far.
There I with yearning sigh
Turn versicular.

Yet worse than that befalls
When gardens grand I view.
I think of my own yard
And projects there to do.

But yards are not estates.
And funds have limits too.
Such facts necessitate
But dreams, not gardens true.

In dreams the old porch rail,
A terrace balustrade.
The little garden trail,
An avenue in a glade.

Birdbath of cement,
For pool ornamental.
Urn so eloquent,
That pot quite rudimental.

An arch in shrubbery
Brings to mind unbidden
A little *jeu d'esprit*,
The folly almost hidden.

Imagination free
Thus lets me sail above
My little gardenry
Which yet remains my love.

Miracles

The One, they say, on water walked apace,
And loaves and fishes multiplied by grace.
To mock cold death who there in triumph reigned
Was reeking Lazarus to life reclaimed.
The sick were healed. The blind were made to see.
Vile demons cast aside and made to flee.
Apart thus rent were nature's strictest laws
That we so dulled by sense might thus have cause
To lift our minds beyond the veil of sight
And know of regions more of life and light.

But were in time and place such wonders true?
Did nature yield, *mirabile dictu*?
The answer matters much for creeds and clerks.
Their claims draw strength from providential works.
The answer matters too for some who doubt,
Whose solid world wonders must rule out.

For me no need to fear those acts of power,
For common marvels stir me every hour
When in the garden 'fore my 'stonished eye
True miracles, unceasing, glorify.

From winter's dark and frigid grave each spring
Dead Lazarus bulbs rise on golden wing.
A few loaves and fishes a hillside fed,
But lavishly one modest plant will spread
Ten thousand seeds o'er waiting ranges far.
A burning bush still glows, a garden star.
And Samson-like, an eyeless root or stalk
Will bring down temples of cement and rock.
Such wonders fill the gardener's dazzled eye,
For miracles flourish through earth and sky.

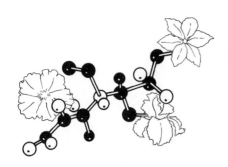

That is to say, for those whose eye can see.
Alas, that there are some who disagree.
Mere chemicals, materialists explain,
By heat and light are moved to turn and change.
As if that illumes anything at all
Of beauty, youth and age, of spring and fall.

Analysis, I hold, can nothing teach
Of that for which the yearning heart will reach.
The garden, then, no place for mind so dense
That will not give to flowers reverence.

The Garden Pleases

In life fast flowing
No thing of good or ill does stay.
Memory, though, and hope,
As calm pools in swift currents,
Give relief and repose.

Joy, fear, pain,
Hard winter, numb grief,
Work to work, paycheck to paycheck,
Life rushes past.

The garden rests.
Sweeping Arboretum bed,
Backyard border,
Window box.
Heart's ease, glowing wonder.

Seasons pass. In the mind's eye
The garden pleases.
Gardens past and gardens planned,
Relief and repose,
Calm pools in a swift river flowing.